WAKE

poems by

Bernard Briggs

Published in 2018 by Bernard Briggs

Designed and Typeset by Lumphanan Press
www.lumphananpress.co.uk

Printed and Bound by Imprint Digital
Upton Pyne, Devon, UK

ISBN: 978-1-9999039-2-3

‘…is it a vision of the individual soul’s journey through time, a passage as transient as a boat’s wake on flowing water?’

– *William Boyd, Any Human Heart*

Contents

Mr Darwin

Just thought you'd like to know
I'm sitting in my truck having a cup of tea.
Across the road, sparrows are pecking dead insects
from the grilles and number plates of parked cars.
Watching evolution.
Thinking of you.

Starling Party

come on
groove chick check out my moves
oh I'm so hot tonight
have you seen my wing-wiggle
tail-shuggle head-bobble leg-jiggle
get down fly around
do you dig my plumage
yeah bring all your friends
we're going to make eggs tonight

Sunday Breakfast

We're facing east, wondering
who scraped the waves from Aberdeen bay,
sat toy boats on a mirror.
Walking south towards Footdee
Saturday night is strewn on the promenade.

A young girl flat-foots along the asphalt
trailing sinews of perfume in the morning air,
side-swipes memories on a smart-phone.
Heels dance on a finger,
beaten eventually from her feet.

Skeletal on a bench
a man stares, squinting at the sun,
daring it to rise further.
Grips flat dregs in a can,
swivelling his rough neck as we pass.

Crows stalk the foreshore
while in the old nightclub doorway
paper-sorting seagulls scatter takeaways.
We head for home chewing bones,
spitting them into the Torry wind.

Gulls

Like discovering a cat
lying across your feet
it takes you by surprise.
Stop-start technology and
a new quietness at traffic lights.

You crack open the car window,
lean your head against the air
and breathe.
The granite echoes
all of a sudden beautiful.

Early Arrivals

leaves arrived this morning
shunned
by the first breath of autumn
resting momentarily
on lawns before
clattering over concrete
searching for corners of winter
to compost

following their progress
we spotted threads of summer
unravelling in the breeze
then looking up at the trees
felt a need to dress them
in gloves hats and scarves
to visit high wardrobe shelves
when we got home

New Year Shift

before dawn
                    my first breath
is a reflex to need
and January   a shelf
thirty-one black books
stacked bracketed
                    numb cold
stretching
down   winter   roads
old spells   long cast
chicken innards   under the moon

driving between brindle verges
bare throated trees
swallow
          my shadow
new year isn't working
          in my head

Jam

The doctor didn't tell me
what cholesterol looks like, or even
what colour it's painting
my arteries' walls.

Not Ferrari red, I suspect, or
British-Racing green.
More like New York taxi-cab
yellow, sweating
in a slow clog of
'get outa my way fella'
all the way downtown.

The doctor did tell me there was
nothing much to worry about,
just ditch the wheels
and walk.

If Someone Had

looked into his eyes
would it have allowed
at the least, some understanding,
moments before that explosion
on a Manchester Monday?

In the second before
he pulled the pin, or whatever it was he did
would they have seen, like an old telly
that pinpoint of light
before disconnection?

Head-wind

up Argyle Place
my legs stutter
bumping into you
sweeping low through the trees
of Victoria Park

you're a bully
shoving me in the chest
as I jog on the spot
impotent head down
trying to ignore you

do me a favour
take your clattering leaves
icy fists and scatty shadows
find another corner
and blow on someone else

Boilings

(Brought in from the shed
the old copper boils laundry;
warms the house with soap-steam.)

In the kitchen I prepare time capsules,
topping and tailing, scrubbing clean,
covering them with salted water and
as they start to bubble in the pan
it's Monday in Sussex, the Sunday roast
relegated to cold flat lamb, slapped
onto cornish-ware plates, waiting
for mashed potato and beetroot.

Saturday Afternoon in a North Facing Garden

tools returned to the shed
hooked between nails
hammered into brick
clean, hard used, easy found next time

house, worked into corners
neat ordered piles
apron hung on larder door
rhythms of baking beside the cooling oven

deck chairs unfolded
placed side by side on the grass
turned pages, tipped china rims
drifting eyes

mum and dad nudged down the lawn
towards the Buddleia
taunted by shadows
muttering exchanges

cursing the half hourly drag
back into the sun

Bed-bound

mum sleeps   six hundred miles
I work, clean floors
sweep dust and grit into piles

mum sleeps   one hundred miles
I drive, her end of life care plan
in my pocket

mum sleeps   ten miles
I think about questions
try to choose words

mum sleeps   two yards
she can't be woken to ask
so, I will have to be her

mum sleeps   there
skin, like story layers
the parchment of her

mum sleeps here
steadying my hand
I sign my love

Winter

You're in the corner, cupped by a chair,
wearing the same old cardigan and skirt.

A dry leaf, one breath
would send out of the window.

I kiss your forehead, your eyes flick open:
'Piss off shit face.'

I smile, remembering when you would
smack my legs for swearing.

Dry

mum's weather is out of reach now
displayed each morning
beyond opening curtains

gossiping clouds above
turning down sheets
adjusting pillows
cleaning the room to a desert
talk weather
chase storms over tea cups
drench conversations
whipping up hurricanes
blizzards tempests
thunder and flood

she can only listen
a drought
remembering the feeling
of rain on her tongue

Trundle Hill

Chalk-Pit lane carves deep
through Sussex turf
up to Trundle Hill.
Kids explore white water cuts,
grassy down-lands,
skylarks slicing the breeze.

They Trek through wool-storms,
bleating in the summer heat.
Den in hollow gorse thickets,
scratch knees on flint floors,
scuff Start-Rites,
playing at doctors and nurses.

Beneath pylons, they run on ancient mounds.
Then, thin legs exhausted, squat
on scorched, nibbled grass,
flicking rabbit currents; taking turns to stab
at landmarks through the haze.
Sails on a distant Solent

When the long sun melts, they
drive their feet through downhill dust,
kicking flint footballs
at fence posts.

On Sundays

We toed the line,
trod Lavant paths
to St Nicholas' or St Mary's.
A rotation of Saxon and Norman.

Inside, pieties of polished oak and brass,
psalms to Pledge and Duraglit.
There was floral jousting; oasis at twenty paces
so God could smell our prayers.

Slicing with his lofted cross
God progressed towards the altar
through frocks, brogues and lavender coats,
de-mob suits and clutched hats.

We felt it, through the seat of our trousers,
the buzz in our ears and on our tongues.
The knot of compliance
never loosened.

Some Faith

Some walked to church,
some drove, even though it was just around the corner.
We walked from the other end of the village,
alongside the river, passing the Rectory.
Flint and rambling roses set back from the lane.

Some kept to the rear pews,
some had named and cushioned ones just below the alter.
We sat on a hard bench, just inside the west door
beneath un-stained windows.
Behind stacks of Ancient and Modern.

Some chose conscience over communion,
some always took it; first to the oak rail.
We considered the queue meandering down the nave,
joining the end if there was time.
If the Rector's sermon had shown mercy.

Some passed the collection plate low along the line,
some made a show of their piety.
We rattled copper between paper and silver,
remembering the lesson about temptation.
Dad held my brother's wrist as he dropped his penny.

Some collected hymn books, surpluses for washing,
some filed past the Rector, touching heaven in the porch.
We placed flowers on Nan's grave and headed home,
alongside the river, passing the Rectory.
Flint and rambling roses set back from the lane.

Talking Hats and Ducks

Dad used to call me Duck.
It was affectionate:
'...that's it Duck; thanks Duck
n-night Duck'.

He called others Duck as well:
my mother and my brother,
anyone he was fond of. He was
a gentle smile of a man.

He also had sayings, like:
'If you want to get a hat, first
you have to get a head'

if I didn't understand.

(or was it ahead?)

He wore a tweed flat cap,
old and frayed, with a finger-greased peak.
He called it his titfer,
said he felt naked without it.

At mealtimes, he would counsel:
'Eat what you can
and can what you can't'
if I was struggling to clear my plate.

In the mornings, when he left
for the Tri-ang toy factory, he'd shout:
'See you later alligator...' and
I'd always reply: '...in a while crocodile'.

(we stole that one from Bill Haley)

If I was ill, he was wise too:
'It isn't the coughing that carries you off
it's the coffin they carry you off in'.
He was right of course.
Still is.

-o-

Bonfires

I inhale leaf-steam,
the curry of charred weeds.

Inhaling deeper (closer),
fifty years and fifty yards
I see my dad and a bonfire
smoking behind a hedge
at the bottom of the garden.

Curling unions of grounsel,
bindweed, campanula,
bramley tree prunings
and Players Navy Cut
drifting up into a horse chestnut haze.

He had a rare skill with embers.
Raking, huffing a glow in the ash,
applying a corner of the Daily Mirror.
Gently building heat, carefully
adding fuel to the flame.
This mattered.

His heaps were smoulder marathons.
Deeply burnt, sometimes
for a week or more, re-piled
each evening after tea.
Heating the night air.

They're long cooled now
but still burning.

-o-

Letters from the Front

Grandad flickers on the back of my eyelids,
pitchfork upright, grey eyes staring,
collarless shirt, sleeves rolled,
big trousers, boots, the regulation moustache,
stiffened upper lip.

He wrote letters to Nan from a trench in Belgium.
His hand like him: strong, quiet.
No mention of bullets and shells.
Keeping them to himself
and his mates in the battalion.

Instead, he wrote about the weather,
iron rations, joy in a wash, clean vest and pants,
the peace that would come by Christmas.

He enquired about the harvest, home and his children.
Always sent his love: three crosses for three kisses.
Sometimes asked for packets of tea, tobacco,
a pocket mirror, shaving stick and blades.

Home, head on shoulders, blood in veins,
limbs and faith in God and king intact.
He never told us about his medal, received for bravery,
pulling a wounded officer from no-man's land.

Small Pieces of Ground

figures stand
soldiers against the sky
survey the ground
they've made, they've lost
they've dug
such small pieces of ground

palms kissing, they
look up, watch clouds gather
enemies advancing
hearts on spears
gaining such
small pieces of ground

as light fades
figures fall
foetal against the mud
shrinking into comrade's arms
they become just
small pieces of ground

Eleven Days

I think of you from time to time.
About how, on December 13th 1949
you arrived too early at the party.

You were unfinished,
not ready, so you left
before the dancing.

I think of you from time to time.
Keep you alive.
Show you sunrises,
hold sweet peas to your nose,
feed you brown toast and honey,
sit beside you in the crease of a smile.

I think of you from time to time.
As Dad must have done,
as Mum may still, in her quiet prison.

Together they invited you.
Believed you to be
the genesis of their family.

For eleven days, you were.

Diamonds

they speak of little now
after sixty years
the aching duty of housework
cobweb hunting, chopping vegetables
watching pots come to the boil

intermittent poetry of sleep
the minutiae of their existence

people gossip about them
of mediocrity, habits and ruts
a barren love
of taking each other for granted
but for years they've feasted on love

wet their lips on it
stuffed their guts

they hold hands
on the way to the supermarket
argue in the aisles
about biscuits, beans and the price of tea
count their money slowly at the till

everyone looks but
no-one sees them shine

Brew

her kettle wakes early
the tea cupboard opening
to a wrist flick eagerness

fingers tapping the door

she considers each brew in her head
scanning the neat packets
knowing every cure

tea, she says

there is no question in the word
no reply expected from me
it just hangs like steam

for the love of it

she selects lemon-grass tea from Nepal
I agree in my head and
the cup arrives, handle swivelling

Cold Cup

stirring again
coffee for one

there was no noise
with this cup
no grinding foreplay
no whisper of cloth
in the stretch for things
no happy chink
or pumpy throb
no union of sighs
just the stillness
of missing   conversation

The Kitchen Table

is the nucleus in our atom
legs turned, nicely fashioned
in robust utilitarianism
right up to the thick   flat timber   top

grace is said at four straight sides
corners are avoided in our twisting days

things arrive in shifts, drifts
of paper, plastic, unfinished business
clatters of porcelain   steel   keys   phones

the heat of sustenance, sometimes subsistence
leaving a mark, a stain with each serving

amongst the seen, the unseen
spitting   thumping   choking
the scoring of points
lines drawn across the wood
squashing of buttocks and backs
smearing sweat into the grain

crumbs scattered
at it's
feet

Fresh

Cling-film
compresses the skin,
accentuates the areas
we've torn off.
They expand under
the lack of surface tension,
two inches
of cool air in the small of my back,
an inch
on the inside of your left thigh.
Unwrapping each other
slowly, we are ready
to serve.

Counting Kisses

Only three kisses.
You sent me
only three kisses.

I sent you five
in my last text
and a smiley face.

Last Tuesday
you sent a six
and a 'love you babe'.

I'm not counting... obviously
but is there something
you're not telling me?

Letter

pinned to a tree, pen prick on your skin
life was pressed into you there and then
making sure everything was written down

rough edges turned by the wind
corners whipping you hung for a week
rain washing words to ink again

the sun crisped your body
until it cracked and fell
you will not be written again

Barn Dance

Straw, I knew, could disappoint
especially when baled.
So when you slowly lead me by the hand
behind the bang and strum of the band
I was hoping for hay.

Instead, in the flashing shadows
our nest was an oily tarpaulin, a stain
beside a disembowelled John Deere.

I was a downy fifth year,
you, a class above me
learning geometry and lipstick.
The hard packed mud vibrated our bones,
straw stalking the crevices between us.

Winter Gardens

From a desert

in Ethiopia, a graffiti-scratched
cactus skin. Freshly cut
under a quartered sun.
Slowly drying.

She leads him

into the Amazon rainforest.
Crushed coloured glass,
dripping stars against green
scattered skies.

Through the exit

back to Aberdeen.
Fingers hooked together,
penknife in her pocket,
folded blade seeping.

Knots in the Weave

From my position on the bed
I see you float from there
to there, to there, as you
remove, discard, gather, arrange
rearrange, apply, reapply yourself.
Then you turn and look at me.

One day you'll tell me how
you do that: ignite lightening
between our closing skins.
Finger-tips almost touching down hair,
our pores call to each other
before you remove the air for breath.

Your cool running mouth moistens
from toes, to thighs, to navel, to neck
and then it is me, afloat but
drowned inside you, as you, with you,
remembering the patterns,
the knots in our weave, so long tied
we will never unpick them.

His

The car park at the Raceway.
Rain, hard enough for cars to swim,
for shoes to fill with water and sink.
My brother, track-side watching one more race.
His green mk1 Ford Cortina standing,
dripping into oily puddles.

Me posing inside, dry in the driver's seat
suddenly awkward, unsure
trying to ignore the white lace
taunting me from the rear view mirror.
His girlfriend, in the back
soaking wet, peeling her clothes.

Blushing, I mumble about his Cat Stevens'
'Teaser and the Firecat' cassette
being chewed up by the car stereo.
Think: the rain, the racing, the bangers
the burgers; anything
but underwear and damp skin.

Seeing in the Dark

late January afternoon
smudged charcoal
drifts into the distance

chained to railings
two stolen wheels leave
a frame waiting for recycling

resting in the road
a Nordmann fir contemplates
tinsel and compost

through the window
trees rubbed to almost nothing
by the room's reflection

Yard

a hundred square metres of concrete and me
sitting watching, with a fly-cup in a car-boot mug

the leaves already paler on the trees
the fields scraped   re-sown   green blushed

this is where I sit, absorbing weather
a corner of autumn   sipping tea   unrolling thoughts

in the field next door, cows chew, suckle calves
I wonder if they read minds
I wonder if they enjoy the view as much as me
the flat, the curved stretched convergence
falling away to the sea

I'm testing the wind
the grass   south-bound geese   silence

I close my eyes, sink
into the vinyl covered seat of the fork-lift-truck

Indian

Below field edge birches
fox pauses, surveys
in a plough's twist
swirls of gull.

Sunrise advances
over damp-field carvings,
dragging long shadows
across brown shire crumb.

The moment breathes
October warmth.
A sneeze and grass re-stands
where once, brindled rust lay.

Describing a Colonsay Sunset

four figures stand in the chill
beaten faces to the west
blushed by the falling day
watching as dusk, continues to form
in discussions of cloud and southern winds
the sun, at this island's edge, is cupped by black rocks
soft flesh, cut hard

somehow it is better outside the house; feels closer
subtracting six yards from infinity
two hold cameras, pouring pictures into silicone cauldrons
butterflies in jars, hummingbirds in cages, rainbows in hands

they've watched sunsets before, even held
entire conversations about
magenta, burnt orange, cerise, aquamarine
but this one, this one
melts wire in eyes, forges steel, cuts blood into the sea
on each line of colour, words are written
washed from the glass sky, staining pages

Great Glen

We are lost in peaty reflections.
The Caledonian Canal
flattened between banks.
No need to look up.

We follow iron and wood,
coal and peat from
Corpach to Clachnaharry,
pulling ropes with muscle voices,
gathering mountains with restless eyes.

We shove worlds away,
throw pebbles, crack mirrors,
gasp at one last lock of black water.
Dive into myths
before resurfacing.

Wake

Oban to Tiree.
West, in the company of Mull
the ferry's wash suggested
pig's stomach lining
or Italian dry cured ham.

It was like that
standing on the deck, watching
our progress dissolve.
It loaded more textures
than I could handle.

But later, distilled gently
by fire and water
I forced a pen to stand.
Pages filled,
becoming my wake.

What We Found With Water

wood and rust, tumbled above black tide scars
twists of rope and hawser
warped shadows, slicing rocks
a sheep's skull, sucked white
after dinner sea-urchins, smashed, empty
abandoned sea houses on moss
wind tugged slaps of sea, warm salt-crust lips
long eyes, unfocused shapes in a far haze
cloud mountains, hill clouds
bladder berries, punctuating warm flat spume
low tide, wet islands and sky
sand hollows, dug by seal boulders
beaches running off to America
tall lumped butts of cliff and
low cranium rocks, splitting surf
hard blue pools, rising light bubbles
glugging, filtering, living
bruises, waiting for deep cool rescue
thrums, scattered in sea weaves
white promenade footprints, back filling with brine
a rough peace, cracking open beneath the sun

Rising Ground

Voices gather
booming under whippy larches.

You could fall in love here,
with this serious land and
every storm splintered tree.

Senses foam,
brewing draughts of sap and peat.

In this wind you could fly from Mither Tap.
The birds, free-falling like water,
singing you home.

On Mither Tap

there is never silence
no nothing always something
there is peace of sorts yes
where sound sulks behind
other hills other horizons
behind trees
under rocks
down
rabbit holes

what is close adjacent
obvious
full on in our faces is the wind
every finger knuckle of granite
every ragged sprig of heather promise of grass and
seated windcheater
sends a howl to a scream a whimper to a moan
bends quiet into bracing

there is never silence here
total silence like total loneliness
but who would want that

at least there's the wind
which sometimes pretends
to be quiet

Fallen

In Glenmore, by the footpath to An Lochan Uaine:
storm scars, skeletal twins, lying pierced by saplings.
Fractured plates of bark stripped from bones
now bleached through years of Cairngorm wind.
They rest between ground elder and heather
on a rusted mat of earth, splintered grain
depening silently each year.

River-fall

Every day
rain permitting
the river's direction is set
by gravity
to run the same course
and as glass
sparkle
under the sun
silvering the forest
bending sky blues
around guiding rocks
flushing rainbow-fish
through tree roots
flowing under shady branches
that every autumn
send boats to the sea.

Orknaeology

Broch:

The fog of heat, heavy with turf-dust.
Boiling roots, roasting meat and fish
guts, slipping into the midden.
The stink of animals,
of human toil, settling fireside.
And embracing it all, a surprising quiet
punctuated by the murmur of wood on bone,
teeth on gristle; the scratching of existence.

Ring:

a small hill leaning
a lochan restless under the wind
witnesses to construction as worship
the act of remembering ghosts
sixty vertical stabs of stone
a ditch picked from bedrock
drawn there by an orbit of rope
a sun and a moon in the heather.

Cairn:

We deflesh. Smell the iron
of beast and clan, the red blood
of hours, in split and stacked sandstone flags.
Dark cut from light, weathered, cracked, broken.
Green algae from cold damp air stains our fingers
as we lay out, pass on, remember, revere.
We bury bones; bodies of them.

-o-

The Whisky Hunters

Smudged against a green-washed Orkney bay
two figures dance in wellington boots.
Harvesters, tangoing across dimples in the sand.

reverse, one – two – fork, bend – spoot – bucket
advance, three – four – fork, bend – spoot – bucket

Striding, stooping, straightening, thrusting,
they search carefully, at ten pounds per dozen,
for every dram on the beach.

Tied

This island crouches.
Rimmed and cracked by sea glass,
a white grainy ruff pulled tight
around its rocky neck.

Cruel westerlies
chew at its fishermen
up to their chests in the loch.
Lashing them with endless waves.

Softening in deep brown hollows
it sends a trout for supper.
Stunned against a bottle bank,
gutted in a flash of silver.

It traps migrants in quay stacked creels.
Claws others back for burials,
forming them into crescents of black.
Washed bones in machair kirkyards.

Map References

We don't need maps on the island, she said:

Tam Mackinnon is the hill you're looking for,
rises up just north east of here.
Bastard of a place; was up there last week
looking for sheep to bring down.
Tam was a mate; sort of a drinking mate
until, we reckon, he drank so much he got lost
out on his quad. He ended up bent backwards
in a gully, his collie sitting next to his head.
I found them and named the place.

Squint-Eyed Will is the really deep lochan
shaped like a fist, just east of Tam.
Will drowned, fishing for trout.
We all told him there were no fish there
but you'd often find him sitting on a rock
line baited and cast, waiting for a bite.
Some like to believe he hooked a big one.
When they dragged him out, it's been said
he had a smile on his face and Gary said:
a deep red gash in the corner of his mouth.
Gary loved him like a brother
so the lochan became Will.

You'll find Bethany Shearer on the west coast,
north of the big beach. A tourist found her body
last July; dressed in black as always.
At first they thought she was a dead seal, but seals
don't wear backpacks covered in gothic symbolism
or have dirty needles sticking out of their flesh.
All the lads loved Bethany, until
she started hitting the drugs. One stuck with her, Tam
he tried to help, but he had his own issues.
This year a lot of the kids held a naming party there.
Some from the island even knew her.

She handed back the map.

-o-

Tiree Bobby

Our walk today
along thread roads
found us saying goodbye
to Bobby.

We didn't know him
but others did.
The parking of cars
on the verge
outside the Kirk
hinted of him
the man; his passing
now lodged with ours.

Inside their straight wooden grief
the mourners did not know
that we'd witnessed
his return to the island.
His island home
now lodged in us.

Anchored

Southbound towards Aberdeen
granite rises beyond sailing dunes
and the North Sea spills
under whale back clouds.

Then a ritual: today we count
twenty-three oil workers
chain down in the bay,
a pilot's call from harbour.

Berthed, their steel spires merge,
tied together by the need
to belong somewhere
when water swallows the sun.

Some of the poems have enjoyed a previous life:

'Anchored' – *previously appeared in Pushing Out the Boat magazine, Issue 14.*

'Boilings', 'Bonfires', 'Bed-bound', 'Saturday Afternoon in a North Facing Garden', 'Eleven Days' *and* 'Dry' – *previously appeared in Fault Lines, a Lemon Tree Writer's publication (2017).*

'On Mither Tap' *and* 'Rising Ground' – *previously appeared in The Leopard Magazine, September 2016.*

'Map References' – *previously appeared in the online magazine The Island Review.*

'Gulls' – *previously appeared in White Wings of Delight, an Elizabeth Reinach/Keith Murray publication, in aid of the RSPB.*

'Great Glen' *and* 'What We Found with Water' – *previously appeared in the San Pedro River review, Vol.7 No.2 (Fall 2015).*

'Small Pieces of Ground' – *previously appeared in Keith Murray's publication Poems for Armistice, 2013.*

N.B. A small number of poems here were written during 2014, in response to prompts issued as part of the '52 project', an online poetry group founded and curated by poet Jo Bell. They were initially shared on the group's Facebook page.

I need to thank a few people:

I could not have written these poems without a bit of help from time to time. In particular I'd like to acknowledge the guidance and critical advice of fellow writers within two groups: Lemon Tree Writers and members of The Apothecary Sessions, in the development of this collection.

I'd especially like to thank Poet and Playwright, Catriona Yule, who cast a very interrogative eye over the text and was not afraid to challenge me; in some cases, helping me to make sense of my own poetry! Her assistance was invaluable in the final stages of production.